You Know Who's
Awesome?

(Not You.)

TED FOX, illustrations by Ryan Hannus

Avon, Massachusetts

Published by
Adams Media, a division of F+W Media, Inc.
57 Littlefield Street, Avon, MA 02322. U.S.A.
www.adamsmedia.com

ISBN 10: 1-4405-3726-7
ISBN 13: 978-1-4405-3726-4
eISBN 10: 1-4405-3893-X
eISBN 13: 978-1-4405-3893-3

Printed in the United States of America.

10   9   8   7   6   5   4   3   2   1

Library of Congress Cataloging-in-Publication Data
Fox, Ted
You know who's awesome? / Ted Fox.
p. cm.
ISBN 978-1-4405-3726-4 (hardcover)—ISBN 1-4405-3726-7 (hardcover)—ISBN 978-1-
4405-3893-3 (ebook)—ISBN 1-4405-3893-X (ebook)
1. Conduct of life—Humor. 2. Popular culture—Humor. I. Title.
PN6231.C6142F69 2012
818'.602—dc23
2012004513

This publication is designed to provide accurate and authoritative information with regard to
the subject matter covered. It is sold with the understanding that the publisher is not engaged
in rendering legal, accounting, or other professional advice. If legal advice or other expert assis-
tance is required, the services of a competent professional person should be sought.
—From a *Declaration of Principles* jointly adopted by a Committee of the
American Bar Association and a Committee of Publishers and Associations

Many of the designations used by manufacturers and sellers to distinguish their product are
claimed as trademarks. Where those designations appear in this book and Adams Media was
aware of a trademark claim, the designations have been printed with initial capital letters.

Illustrations by Ryan Hannus

This book is available at quantity discounts for bulk purchases.
For information, please call 1-800-289-0963.

Introduction

Do you ever stop and think: "Everyone is just so awesome"?
Me neither.

In fact, if you're like me, you're constantly amazed at how un-awesome people can be. I'm talking about *all* people, myself included. The girl I asked out via an eight-page letter back in college can vouch for that. (I swear it seemed like a good idea at the time.)

Of course, it's not as if the grown man riding a skateboard down the sidewalk or the coworker reeking of tuna yet offering unsolicited fashion advice are the only ones reminding us something in this great experiment called "life" has gone terribly awry.

There are famous people, who by definition have to be at least a little crazy.

There are businesses that make us wish we could go back to an economy based on barter.

And there are cats.

Now unlike my better judgment, the obnoxious prove hard to ignore. That's why I decided to fall back on the best weapon I have: irony. It's less sad when you don't think about it too hard.

Not just any kind of irony would do. No, if I planned on getting way too emotionally invested in things of little to no consequence, I wanted to do it big, taking a ubiquitous word typically reserved for exclamations of joy and turning it on its pretty little head. And so I asked, gazing off into nowhere:

"You know who's *awesome?*"

I'll let you know when I run out of answers.

The author of *Grieving for Dummies.*
"At a loss for words? Give the gift that says 'I'm so sorry you're too stupid to appreciate your loss.'"

Restaurant claiming something on its menu is "famous." First clue you might be lying: I walked here from a Days Inn.

Cadillac stopping traffic to wait for a parking spot. Have these people honking gone mad? It's not your fault the mall didn't build a wider aisle.

Wine snobs. 10 bucks says you'd pick the box of Franzia in a blind taste test.

Wearers of camouflage-themed sports gear. Afraid things are going to get a little dicey between the couch and the bathroom?

Grooms who don't get it. Piece of advice: Find that sweet spot between "He's not helping," and "He's insisting we get married at Buffalo Wild Wings."

The Big 10 and the Big 12. Counting your teams is harder than it looks.

People who wait in line for 10 minutes at McDonald's only to agonize over their order when they get to the front of the line. How many times have you been here? It's not like you're choosing between the prime rib and the tilapia in the lemon butter. Pick your McNuggets or your Big Mac and get on with your life.

People who don't lock single-toilet public restrooms. This is one gamble where we all lose.

Priest working from an iPad. "Even in our grief, we can see that . . . Sr. Sue just became mayor of the parish on Foursquare? Well that sucks."

Frank Sinatra. What kind of shit *were* you getting into if you didn't think you'd get a "kick" out of cocaine?

DJ Hero **DJ who thinks he's now quali-fied to DJ for real.** I'm under no such delusion. Though I do come correct on the 1s and 2s. Trust, son.

Friends of the middle urinal. "Splash zone" shouldn't be used anywhere but a Gallagher show, which means it shouldn't be used anywhere.

Hosts of webinars. An hour of learning nothing has never felt so vaguely informative.

The screenwriter of *Air Bud*. This dog likes to play basketball with a little kid? Please. Now if it were baseball with Matt LeBlanc, I might buy it.

Awkward award show presenters. Even Joe Biden just got uncomfortable.

Women wearing overly furry boots.

Looking like you assaulted a Yeti? Yeah, that's not hot.

Strangers who volunteer how much their stuff cost. $400 for those jeans? Wow. You wouldn't think they'd make you look so trashy.

U2 fans talking about Bono like he's Jesus. We get it—he's a great dude. But that's all he is: a dude. In some douchey glasses.

People who get up as soon as the plane comes to a complete stop. What makes this so efficient is that only 99 percent of the flight thinks to do it.

Guy getting hit in the head by a closing parking gate. Can't we all just be thankful I didn't suffer a concussion?

GEICO. If our intelligence relative to Neanderthals ever goes on trial, we better pray that sitcom about the caveman is ruled inadmissible.

That guy wearing the Bluetooth headset during the staff meeting. Gee whiz, mister! You must be a real big deal to have a cell phone in your pocket!

Grumpy neighbors who "haven't been home" the last five Halloweens. Good to know your beef isn't with me specifically but rather life in general.

John Mayer. Your songs make me think you really do care about me. But I know better.

Assholes. We know it. You know it. Everybody knows it. And yet we all get to pretend we don't. Hooray.

Non-cowboys wearing cowboy hats.
You haven't seen a buffalo anywhere but in front
of "wings."

RV driver ignoring the "Left Lane Closed Ahead" sign. Just nudge your way in when you get to the flashing arrow; really, it's okay. Sitting in traffic for 15 minutes so you can get to the Yogi Bear campground a little faster has been the bright spot of this otherwise tedious road trip. By all means, invite your friends, too. You're all welcome here, which as near as I can tell, is located somewhere between mile marker 17 and the fourth circle of hell.

Drivers who voluntarily give up the right of way but then get impatient waving the other car through the stop sign. I'd hate to see birthdays at your house.

"Thank you for the gift, Nana. I love the way you wrapped . . ."

"Just open the fucking box already, motherfucker."

Little kids in horror movies. I didn't need to see you crawl through the TV to convince me being a parent is terrifying.

The Easter Bunny. If East Germany taught us anything, it's that no one gets that big just by "working out."

Guy talking about his "man card" in his "man cave." The lady doth protest too much, methinks.

Rage Against the Machine. Maybe try "Healthy Indignation Against the Machine." Your blood pressure has to be through the roof.

Whoever decided every cause gets a ribbon. Diseases, the troops, I get it. Bowhunters' rights? Not so much.

***Price Is Right* contestants who bid one dollar.** Let me guess: You were the kids who reminded the teacher when she forgot to assign homework, too.

Uncle Jesse. The one from *Full House*, not *The Dukes of Hazzard*. "Have mercy" got old real quick. Overalls, on the other hand, are timeless.

TV shows desperate to trend.
#losingsomething #whenyouplugit #onscreen

Guy parking his ride across two spots in the Target parking lot 50 feet away from any other cars. That is one pimpin' . . . Acura?

Midlevel managers who attend meetings they don't need to. "Sorry I'm late; I got held up over in marketing." "We're accountants." "You'd be surprised by how much I have to say on subjects I know little to nothing about."

Lousy tippers. If you can't afford to leave 15 percent of a Chili's bill, you can't afford Chili's.

Shoppers who leave their carts in parking spots. Who can blame you? That cart corral is a good 7 feet away.

Psycho Little League parents. "See the shortstop? That's my boy. Arm like Jeter. Only eats egg yolks. Hard to believe he'll be six in June."

House Hunters couple complaining that the bathroom doesn't have his-and-her sinks. "Pet cemetery out back, okay, but I won't wait to spit out Plax."

People who point out typos on menus. Is your life so boring that commenting on a misplaced apostrophe in the description of the chicken fried steak actually seems interesting? Or is it just some sick obsession with always being right, even when you're hungover at a Denny's and still wearing pajamas?

It's kind of a tossup for me. Either way, I like to think I'm providing a public service.

John Hancock. If there had been office birthday cards in 1776, you would've been the guy who signs half the left side.

Male flight attendant in shorts. The terms on Priceline didn't say anything about your leg hair being above my tray table.

Personal injury attorneys. Ad during *General Hospital*? Check. 800 number? Check. Aggressive finger-pointing by out-of-work actor? Check. I'm sold.

Stock market analysts. And here I thought predicting the future based on the shape of sheep entrails was a dead art.

Dude convinced the Hooters waitress is into him. That's like Snape thinking he had a shot with Lily Potter.

Lady holding her cell phone between her boobs. There's no punch line. You really are awesome.

Ann Coulter. I would've gone "The power of Christ compels you" route, but I'm guessing you'd think He's too liberal.

US Weekly. Come to think of it, I bet stars *are* really just like us.

Bride getting a tattoo in her wedding dress. Over/under on the *Springer* appearance: 1.5 years.

Men with neck tattoos. At least we know where we can get a shank.

Guy calling his wife "dude." Did "ass-munch" seem a little too crass?

Britney Spears. Just went back and listened to "If U Seek Amy." I'm starting to think it wasn't actually about trying to find someone.

Baseball fans waving at the camera.

Anyone watching who does know you is pretending
that they don't.

Clueless play-by-play announcer. "I can't tell you why there's a flag on the field because I'm too busy making an unnecessarily hyped call of a seven-yard, first-quarter run in the hopes that some ESPN production assistant will hear it and include me in the *SportsCenter* highlight.

"And now—mascot puns!"

Fan who hates an athlete for going to a new team for more money. Because I'm sure your loyalty to your own employer runs deeper than a check.

Sky Mall. Although if I ever were going to be open to learning more about a necktie that inflates to become a pillow, it would be during an in-flight presentation of *Bad Girls Club New Orleans.*

Bill Maher. Someone told me you've got it all figured out. Now who was that? That's right—it was you.

Professional poker players. I can't trust anyone who's turned the lyrics of a Kenny Rogers song into a personal mission statement.

The old lady at the next video poker machine. You just lit up to try to knock me off my heater. Little do you know my Tuesday is wide open.

Old Country Buffet. I don't know what they were eating in the old country, but it wasn't five-gallon vats of JELL-O.

Motorcycle rider with a red Mohawk on his helmet. Way to let Sparta down. Turn *300* into *301 Plus a Kawasaki*, and we're all speaking Greek now.

People who say "epic." *The Iliad* was epic; the time you drank a fifth of Jack and thought you were Christopher Walken was not.

Facebook friends. Provided everyone keeps a safe distance.

Sports fans who do the wave. Quick, what's the score? Eh, it doesn't really matter, does it? The real action is in the stands!

E-mailers who overuse emoticons. The frequency with which I :) has cost me more than one job. okay, not really. But I kinda judge them for hiring me.

Stores that advertise free wireless only to deliver it at dial-up speeds. Web access is not a God-given right. But if you're going to trumpet "Free WiFi" on some decal in your front window like you're NBC announcing Jay Leno's return to *The Tonight Show*, then I'm going to feel justified in my semi-douchey, I-need-Internet-that-performs-like-it's-2012 expectations.

Damn. That analogy really isn't helping my case.

People who make up and/or misuse words in an effort to sound smart. "Now granted, I'm genericizing, but you know this 'You know who's awesome?' guy has to be a total loser. How could being awesome be bad? It doesn't make sense; it's nonsensuous."

Snooki. You've gotten more people to read your book than will probably ever read mine. And I'm totally okay with that. Totally. Now please excuse me while I go scream at some pigeons.

Clubber still dancing at the urinal. The Far East Movement never stops for you, even though you shouldn't have boarded the G6 to begin with.

Snapple. Love your drinks, but the "Real Fact" thing is slowly driving me insane. Can I recharge rechargeable batteries 1,000 times or not?

Charlie Sheen. Most actors only have hyena blood. I hear Jon Cryer is a meerkat.

Best Buy. Thanks for letting us browse before we buy it on Amazon.

The cartoon man on the "Caution: Wet Floor" sign. You should learn to be more careful. That floor's always wet.

Fans of "Bobby" De Niro. The two of you are on a first-name basis? I guess I just assumed he wouldn't know someone rocking a pair of Zubaz.

Traveler buying *Hustler* at the airport newsstand. Just keep your hands where I can see them, buddy. On second thought, don't.

Drunk guy passed out on a woman he doesn't know. Postwedding shuttle bus 1, chances of getting laid 0.

The man pacing up and down his driveway in nothing but boxers. Or is this just my neighborhood?

Donald Trump. Some might say your sense of self-importance knows no bounds, but how could it? You know there'd be no shutting them up if *their* private 757 had been the one to give the Wright Brothers a hard-on from beyond the grave.

The makers of Viagra. I don't see how three and a half hours would be any less distressing than four.

Keynote speakers. "Good morning. You've never heard of me, but for the next 90 minutes, I'll be talking to you about my area of expertise, something only vaguely related to a job that is most likely crushing your very soul. Also, please note that following my presentation, I'll be out in the lobby signing copies of my book, which I'm told is even more boring than the address I'm about to give.

"Let's get started."

Hotels that say the movie title won't appear on the bill. Call me crazy, but the $16.99 might give away it wasn't *Dolphin Tale*.

Onlinebootycall.com. Get ready to check Maury telling you "You *are* the father" off your bucket list.

Tourists wearing a shirt of the city they're still visiting. It's possible to ♥ NY without openly begging it to mug you.

Producers of movie opening-credit sequences. Most films would be meaningless if it weren't for those five minutes of disjointed, artsy zooming.

Self-proclaimed members of the Mile High Club. 1. You can't do math. 2. You're full of shit.

Mac haters. Go ahead and tell me I'm a victim of marketing. Oh wait—you can't. Your PC just froze. Again.

Abercrombie & Fitch. "Hey pal, no shirt, no shoes, no service. Oh, I'm sorry; you work here."

Kid wearing an Abercrombie lacrosse shirt. What was your mascot again? Right—the posers.

Early adopters of texting acronyms. You've done more to damage literacy than the entire *E! True Hollywood Story* roster combined.

20-handicap playing from the back tees. Waiting for the green to clear on this par four is wise; your power fade will eat up that 60 degree dogleg.

People who write on the walls in public restrooms. It's a tragedy such genius can be shared only by those who pee the same way you do.

Inventor of the Shake Weight. Did you see someone eating a banana and think, "I can come up with an activity more unintentionally sexual than that"?

State namers. Kind of mailed it in on West Virginia, didn't ya?

Ulysses S. Grant. I guarantee this happened at least once: "You think my name's crazy? Have you met my VP? Schuyler Colfax? I'm not even sure how I'm supposed to pronounce that, and I'm the guy's boss.

"Alright, who's doing shots?"

Highway strip club. Your "All of the liquor, none of the clothes" billboard offends me. I expect more creativity from people in the arts.

Coworker who brags about his "system" for picking NCAA tournament games. A 12–5 upset, you say? Does Vegas know about this?

The designer of espn.com. It looks like the entire Internet just got violently ill in my Safari window.

Celebrities who give their kids crazy-ass names. Hate to spoil your first parent-teacher conference, but GizmoDuck Flip-Flops is going to need counseling.

Duck Sauce. Hello there. Wikipedia tells me you're the "American-Canadian DJ duo" responsible for "Barbra Streisand."

No, not the singer/actress—the song/not really.

You see, dropping a beat and saying "Barbra Streisand" at regular intervals does not, technically speaking, make any sense. Sure, I could just be too old to get you. After all, I still remember where I was when *Gilmore Girls* got cancelled.

Wait, what?

The point is, real music has guts. It has soul. It has artists with $ in their names. Until you understand that, you're never going to meet with any mainstream success.

Guys who wear shoes without socks. You have to smell it when you take them off. Yes, that. It's like you sublet a room to Swamp Thing.

Line cutters. For someone who missed, let's see, 17 of us standing here, you sure didn't seem to have any problem spotting the last piece of salmon.

Pushy salespeople. Us: "Where can I find the lamps?" You: "You look like you could use a new sofa." Us: "Nope, just a lamp." You: "A sectional!"

Semi drivers. I know I couldn't do your job, but I seem to have that in common with at least 50 percent of you. C'mon, dawg—pick a lane.

Actors in Old Navy commercials. I haven't been this terrified of smiley people since Soundgarden's "Black Hole Sun" video.

Real people, not actors. Now that you're in so many TV ads, I have to ask: Does this mean Arnold is, in fact, a terminator?

My fellow Italians who rag on the Olive Garden. No one's saying it's Little Italy; we're just saying the breadsticks are friggin' delicious.

Cabby who spends the entire ride bitching about going to that destination.

Perhaps you shouldn't be driving people around for a living.

Coworker who offers unsolicited fashion advice. Evidently reeking of tuna has qualified you to be the next Joan Rivers.

Whoever put a paper towel in the urinal. The dispenser is way over by the sink, so this was purposeful. What purpose is anybody's guess.

Men who've watched a marathon of *The Hills* on TV Guide Network. Others laughed, but I felt the rain on my skin. And no one else could feel that for me. No one.

Professors with passive-aggressive office hours. Nothing like pregaming with some transcendentalism.

Twitter sluts. Sure, following everyone you can is the easiest way to get love back. But do you even know my name? Huh? Do you?

Drunk mom dancing with her preteen daughter at a restaurant's bar. The key is you *both* know the words to "S&M." It's embarrassing otherwise.

The creator of anti-spam word verification. Did you and the predictive text guy get 75 percent there and then just decide "Fuck it—let's get high"?

This club. It can't even handle me right now.

That coworker no one can completely trust. 90 percent of me says you would love that impression of our boss; 10 percent thinks you want my office.

**Boss who says "Let's try that again,"
no matter how energetic the "Good
morning."** You should know we only flash mob if
it's on PowerPoint.

**Writer using a tablet and stylus to jot
notes.** In my defense, I had left my laptop at home.
Why not pen and paper? Okay, grandpa.

***Family Feud* contestants.** "Clarissa, it's all up to you. Two strikes against your family, one answer left on the board. For the win—give me something that you plug into the wall."

"Clarissa, if you blow this $694 for us . . ."

"Dad, stop pressuring me. Uh . . . a light bulb?"

"A light bulb? Not a lamp, but a light bulb? You're worse than grandpa, and he thinks it's 1979."

TV hosts who say "Welcome back." We didn't go anywhere. Believe us, we wish we had. 10 minutes with the Game Show Network makes us less human.

Merv Griffin. You gave us *Jeopardy!*, which, while amazing, is a punctuation nightmare. Look: I just had to go !,. Yikes—it's getting worse.

Inappropriately dressed mourners. Funeral Going 101: When the family starts a sentence "In lieu of sending flowers," it rarely ends "wear your Hawaiian shirt."

Dudes who do yoga. Your downward dog is indistinguishable from your plank. Or so I heard. It's not like I know the difference. Shut up.

High fivers. Unless one of us has just hit a game-winning shot, hop in your DeLorean and head back to 1985.

Coworkers getting salty at a Q&A. Administrator guy: "Yes, there in the back."

There in the back: "I was just wondering if you had ever considered giving all of us raises while reducing our work week to 20 hours. I mean, in case you haven't noticed, we're totally worth it."

Administrator guy: "Well, that certainly is an . . . interesting suggestion, but unfortunately, I don't know that I could ever justify it to the board, especially in this economy. Thank you, though. Over on the right—you have a question?"

Over on the right: "Not so much a question as a statement. I just find it a little insulting to hear you say we're not totally worth it."

Administrator guy: "Whoa—I'm sorry if I misspoke, but it was most definitely not my intention to suggest . . ."

Undisclosed location: "Oh, so now we're stupid?"

People who give 110 percent. You can't compare to those giving 150 percent, though. And don't even get me started on those who give 207 percent.

Lone picketer reading a book. Your dedication is exceeded only by your apathy.

The federal government. Do us all a favor and sign up for a Dale Carnegie course or something. There's got to be a group rate.

Semi doing 66 to pass one going 65. Old people with walkers on their way to make Nativity scenes out of macaroni overtake each other faster.

Wedding planner using Starbucks to meet with brides. Why don't you get a real office and stop blocking the one available power outlet so I can plug in and get some work done? I'm trying to make a living here, lady.

Stores that say their websites are "open" 24 hours. Is there anyone still confused about how the Internet works?

Cash4Gold. Tell you what: Why don't you send me the money first, and I'll figure out how much jewelry that buys you.

Angry bloggers. Remember when the only platform for your misinformed political rants was family gatherings? Thank goodness we remedied that.

That one kid who always ruined two-player *Contra*. "Stop running ahead and killing me! We're on the same team! Nintendo has changed you, man."

Guy with the $5,000 system in the $500 car. Your bass may be bangin,' but your doors sound like sadness.

Neighbor leaving his Christmas lights up indefinitely. It seems you're too lazy to take them down but not so lazy you won't turn them on each night. In other words—the perfect storm.

Dude with the "I need tickets" sign. Have you asked the guy 2 feet behind you? Because he has like 20. And you seem to be on a first-name basis.

Notre Dame football fans. Are our expectations almost always unreasonable? Is the pope . . . yeah, we've heard that one, too.

Partygoer wearing the "friend with benefits" T-shirt. There's no health screening to get started. It might not be a bad idea in the morning, though.

People who say "Rap? You mean . . . crap?" *Saved by the Bell* called; it wants its idea of a well-crafted insult back.

Guys who flex. See you at the GNC. Wait, that's not right. What I meant to say was: Gross.

People without headphones playing music on the train. Shorty's got Apple Bottom jeans *and* boots with the fur? Maybe she can lend you some earbuds.

Dude lip-syncing to his headphones.
You're only allowed to do this when a song is the heat.
An example? Uh, ever hear of everything by Beyoncé?

People riding the shuttle to a casino on Good Friday. Trust me, I only got on to judge you.

Lil Wayne. This has been censored for my own good.

The visionaries behind *The Fast and the Furious* franchise. Five scripts using no more than the words "yo," "bro," and "cars"? Respect.

Carmakers that bullshit us on the speedometer. I don't know what's more offensive, Kia—that you defiled Black Sheep's "The Choice Is Yours" with a commercial starring hoodie-wearing gerbils or that you expect us to believe anyone has ever done 140 in a Soul.

People who wear NASCAR jackets. I'd like to thank the DuPont-Chevrolet team for reminding me why I shop at the Gap.

Guy staring at the fountain drinks like he's cracking the Da Vinci Code. "Diet Coke or Coke Zero. Coke Zero *or* Diet Coke". Well-played, Sbarro.

People lingering in the only big, semi-circular booth in a breakfast place on a Sunday morning—with the coffee they brought with them from Starbucks—even though the line out the door is right in front of them. Whatever conversation you're having, it's not that interesting—unless the topic turns to "Hey, we may be the rudest people we've ever met." Then you're probably onto something.

LMFAO. WTF?

Bike riders with headphones. Turn down
the Phish, and you just might discover a whole host of
signs besides "Share the Road."

Guy watching *Footloose* on his iPad in a non-empty, non-crappy restaurant. And why wouldn't you turn it up? There's no game called Six Degrees of Man at the Next Table Proposing to His Girlfriend.

Guy repeatedly requesting the live entertainment "play some 3 Doors Down." Even 3 Doors Down doesn't get it.

Plaintiffs on *The People's Court.* "This is the plaintiff. He says a man he *thought* was his friend asked to borrow his food dehydrator to make apple chips for the birthday party of a mutual acquaintance. However, when the apple chips were a huge hit, the man neglected to share the spotlight and instead claimed it was *his* dehydrator that had produced the delicious snacks. The plaintiff gave his friend a chance to correct the lie but was told, in no uncertain terms, 'What?' Distraught, he fled the party and was forced to eat cereal for dinner. Unbeknownst to him, the expiration date on the milk had been 10 days earlier.

"He's suing for $5,000."

Masseuse working out of her house.

(Massage Table + Adjacent Bedroom) x Canola Oil = "This isn't what it looks like, honey."

Drivers who peel out. We already know your '96 Tercel is the shit; now you're just bragging.

Douchey teenagers. "Dude, I totally made that middle-aged woman uncomfortable by staring at her and saying, 'Really?' I run this food court."

Adults fascinated by revolving doors. It's not a Tilt-A-Whirl; it's the entrance to an office building. Titillation goes here to die.

Husband admiring the newfound definition in his pecs while unknowingly wearing his wife's T-shirt. I really did look good, though.

Home-plate umpires. I long to have a job where I can pretty much be as wrong as I want as long as I do it consistently.

The Real Housewives. Why should a little thing like meaning limit how you use adjectives?

ESPNU. Televised coverage of high school basketball? In July? It's like you're reading my mind.

Defensive lineman running with an incomplete pass like it's a fumble. Give it up. These officials are highly trained . . . alright, I see your point.

Same-side eaters. Your love may be a beautiful thing, but from here, it just looks like the jalapeño poppers are getting you a little horny.

Drivers who back into parking spots.

This takes talent. Like the ability to ignore that everyone watching has figured out you're a tool.

Lady who asks to see your iPad and then, upon realizing it's not a Kindle, says, "Oh, I hate Apple." Glad you could stop by.

People who tackle serious issues with their bumper stickers. Who needs dialogue when you can exhaust your talking points in five words or less?

The American Kennel Club. Your website informs me "Doggy bitches and bitchy dogs are to be faulted." Snoop will not be pleased.

Competitive Monopoly players. "Your two railroads for Baltic. C'mon, it's a great deal. No? Your loss—you just landed there. Four dollars. Pay up, bitch."

Name droppers. Holy shit! You sat next to Tom Bergeron on a plane? And yet you're here talking to me?

Bloggers who "like" their own posts. Do I regret making this decision? Maybe. But when Facebook was still telling me to "Be the first of your friends to like this" several days after I wrote it, I naturally assumed there must have been some sort of problem with the button.

That seemed to be the only reasonable conclusion, anyway.

Guy blaming a reality TV habit on his wife. Say it with me: I keep up with the Kardashians instead of *SportsCenter*. You don't? Uh, me neither.

Chipotle. I won't deny that your fajita burritos are damn-near orgasmic if you'll admit you're a little smug for a fast-food chain.

Restaurants that make us pull the bathroom door open from the inside. And look—a hand dryer in place of paper towels. You bunch of sadists.

The ice cream man. Every time, I think "Today's the day my rocket pop won't need an hour to thaw." Damn you and your siren song.

Enthusiastic conference goers. If you start one more sentence "My colleagues and I," I'm going to go Gary Busey on your ass.

School getting uppity with its honor-roll bumper sticker. All your students are "honorable"? It's junior high, not *Gladiator*.

PhD holders who insist on being called doctor. Why didn't you mention you can quote Aristotle? That is just like open-heart surgery.

Charles Dickens. You published *Great Expectations* way back in the 1860s, but it's still just as boring today.

Garden gnomes. It's obvious you use your magic for ill. How else do you explain the impaired judgment of those buying you?

Lawn care professionals. Saying "Your lawn needs to be fed, sir" like you're calling in a hit probably isn't the best way to get my address.

Mannequins. That blank stare's just a bit too sinister.

Parents on MTV's *Parental Control.* The only thing sadder than your son's loser girlfriend is seeing you talk trash to your son's loser girlfriend.

Women with "Goddess" bumper stickers. Nice pink velour tracksuits.

Alumni who can't let go. "Yes, sir, I know they didn't used to let girls live in this dorm, but it's 6:30 in the morning, and your plaid pants are scaring people."

**Thirty-something-year-old men who con-
stantly quote *Seinfeld*.** Not that there's anything wrong with that.

They. Our dads feel the need to keep us up-to-date
on what you're saying now even though we don't have
a clue who you are.

Freshman-year roommate who shows up with a Ouija board. The only thing you're channeling is awkward conversation.

Cats. It's not like you're secretly wishing us harm.
I think you're pretty up-front about it.

Keanu Reeves. Looking like you understand your lines is overrated.

Fake celebrity tweeters. You're this generation's Elvis impersonators, minus the white jumpsuit and any semblance of marketable talent.

Willem Dafoe. I think dressing as the Green Goblin actually made you less creepy.

Incessant cougher boarding the plane.
Inevitably, you creep closer, and I'm unable to run,
like in that dream where Andrew Jackson is trying to
kill me.

Salesman who asks for a customer's name and then gets it wrong. I don't recommend going all in with: "It was Chris, right?"

Men who don't wash their hands after peeing. Ladies, I'll level with you: The number is mind-boggling. Your boyfriend, though—he's different.

Companies that use celebrity voiceovers in ads. Ooh, I know that guy. It's . . . Denis Leary. No, wait. Bob Saget? Cookie Monster? Dammit.

Spider-Man. If your "Spidey Sense" is tingling, I'd suggest something other than a formfitting unitard.

King Arthur. The eye contact among 100+ guys seated at a round table? Awkward city.

Bob Dylan. Still not getting it.

Streakers at a baseball game. "Aaaaand down the stretch they come! It's On My 12th Beer out in front, followed closely by I'm Just A Dumbass and My Dumbass Friends Dared Me To!

"As for Common Sense, he still hasn't left the gate and appears to be . . . yes, I can confirm that he is indeed shitting himself."

Random businesses with Facebook pages. "Liking" that Holiday Inn Express isn't just for when everywhere else is booked anymore.

Bing. I don't know why Google is better, but I don't know why Kleenex is better than facial tissue, either. It just is.

Automated customer service reps. Hey,
I, Robot: I'm pressing zero to speak with a real person,
so you can stick that in your mainframe and . . . What
do you mean you don't understand that command?
That's the universal code for operator.

No, I don't need to hear the whole menu again.
Here. ZE-RO.

Oh, now I appear to be having trouble? Did you ever
stop to think that someone's question might not fall
under "Press one for billing" or "Press two to sched-
ule new service," you self-righteous piece of shit? Of
course not. You're a computer; you can't think for
yourself.

See you in hell.

Fast food employees who put out a tip jar. The line has to be drawn somewhere, and I'm drawing it when I can see a drive-thru. Judge me if you must.

People who say they wouldn't quit their jobs if they won the lottery. Hold still while I pimp-slap you with this HR manual.

TMZ. If entertainment news outlets were sexual partners, no one would get with you without double-baggin' it.

Girl going home with The Situation. I see the walk of shame is starting a couple of hours early tonight.

Women who don't shave their pits.

No one's saying it's not a double standard; it is.
So we agree. Now may I suggest the Gillette Venus?

Men over 50 with an earring. You see the boat, way out there in the distance? That's your ship sailing.

Women over 50 with bare midriffs. You see the boat, way out there in the distance? That's your ship sailing. And the crew vomiting off the side.

Women whose jackets match their jeans.

Too . . . much . . . denim. And the cross-stitched Tigger isn't helping.

Runner on first. We all know baseball gets slow, but how long do you and the first baseman really need to spend catching up? It's not *The View*.

Know-it-all sports fans who ironically know less than all. Here's an example: "It's 3rd and short. Why don't we run a reverse?"

Deep-voiced preview guys. In a world where the only rule is there are no rules, this week's *House* can't be that big a deal.

People who use "literally" when they mean "figuratively." Because if you really can eat a horse, I'm bringing you a Clydesdale and watching.

People with bad vanity license plates. Hey "YODA": Is that a lightsaber in your trunk, or are you just happy you're not still a virgin?

Pickup truck owners with what's supposed to look like a man's nuts dangling below the back bumper. That description pretty much covers it.

Suburban kids who claim to be from the city. I repped Detroit the first three months of college. Detroit was not amused.

DiGiorno. No shit it's not delivery; it's been in my freezer since February.

Birds that poop on cars. The whole world is your toilet; exercise a little discretion.

Robin picking at a worm on the sidewalk. This may be nature's way, but nature is frequently disgusting.

Drivers who think all lanes are the same. Cross parallel lines with a transversal, and you'll see some interesting properties; cross parallel lanes with a Trans Am, and you'll need to find the gas.

Dude kickin' game while playing '80s music bingo. Naming a Tears for Fears song after three notes and getting her number are mutually exclusive activities.

The director of *Eat, Pray, Love.* I may have come to see Julia Roberts eat gelato, but I stayed to watch her take deep, cleansing breaths. Bra-vo.

People who clap after movies. THE ACTORS CAN'T HEAR YOU.

Pompous hybrid owners. If a polar bear does show up at your door, it won't be to thank you on behalf of the icecaps.

White people with dreads. Just stop it. You know we can't pull it off.

Subaru. Just saw your old truck/car, the Baja, which, if memory serves, was marketed as being "a little less ugly than the Aztek."

Unrepentant sleeptalkers. If I didn't say I was sorry, my wife might leave me. And I wouldn't blame her. Those vows said nothing about Parseltongue.

Neighbor's dog that won't quit barking.
I shouldn't blame you, but Milli Vanilli shouldn't have
blamed it on the rain, either. It happens.

Authors who start a book with a random quote. Thanks for all the context; it really makes the words come alive.

Time travelers. If you spoil how Ted Mosby finally meets those kids' mother, I swear I'll . . . you son of a bitch.

Old hippies. You still remember the set list from a Dead show in Des Moines in 1971? Did weed not work the same way back then?

Condescending coworkers. Seems that master's degree I'm always hearing about didn't teach you that "caveat" and "repeat" don't rhyme.

Coach obsessed with hustle. "Hustle up, guys. I said hustle! Yes, you. Why aren't you hustling? Hustle is my religion, and you're all atheists!"

People who say, "I'll sleep when I'm dead." Fine. But if you wake up, Stephenie Meyer isn't going to be there to help us see your good side.

Teen vampires. As tense as human/undead relations are, devoting a section of Barnes & Noble to "Teen Paranormal Romance" is not the answer.

Tour guides on college campuses. If ever there were an industry in need of regulation, it's one where 19-year-olds have free rein to tell busloads of old people: "And if you look to your right, you'll see a bench, which was a gift from the government of France to commemorate the 100th anniversary of beer pong."

Golf commentators. I appreciate your unrelenting faith in my ability to digest the complex minutiae of a professional golfer's swing. Really, I do.

But here's the thing: I spend more time counting up my strokes after I putt out than I do calculating 15 percent of $29.92 after dinner; what exactly do you expect me to take away from a super slo-mo view of Rory McIlroy's hands at impact? That I suck at golf?

Because I figured that out a while ago.

AOL users. Then again, Gmail would probably crash your Commodore 64.

Guy wearing the "Proud to be awesome" T-shirt. It would appear I'm not the only one playing fast and loose with that term.

Coworker who comes to a meeting an hour late and asks a question that's already been answered. Good thing you didn't hit the snooze a seventh time.

Toms who spell it "Thom." Apparently you were eating paste the day *Sesame Street* was brought to you by the letter H.

Whoever decided to spell "rhythm" that way. "Rhy" and "Thm" aren't syllables; they're characters in a Tolkien novel.

Someone who still has a Rudolph nose on her car in June. I wouldn't go bragging about it in December, either.

Customers who berate cashiers. Don't let the minimum wage fool you; we all know who's in charge around here.

Saps who tear up over pop songs. Unless it's P!nk's "F**kin' Perfect." Or "Defying Gravity" from *Wicked*. And that song that was in *Once*. Excuse me.

New parents incapable of talking about anything but being new parents. If you're looking for more than an "Aww, you must be excited," you've grossly overestimated the impact this information will have on my day-to-day life.

Person 2 in the following conversation. Person 1: "Hey." Person 2: "Hay is for horses!" Person 1: "Eat shit and die."

Baby at an R-rated movie. Of course, I'd be crying if I had your parents, too.

Woman with a "No boyfriend, no problem" T-shirt. Not to be a dick, but it kinda seems like it is.

Coors Light. "The world's most refreshing beer"? That's your slogan? Are we drinking it from a Gatorade cooler during a 20-second time-out?

Burger King's King. Look, what the Swedish Chef and the Joker do on their own time is their business, but their love child isn't selling me on the Whopper.

Scooby Doo **villains.** You would've gotten away with it if it hadn't been for those pesky kids? The ones driving around in the used van? With their talking dog? While they get high? Like all the time?

Yeah, you almost pulled it off.

The Black Eyed Peas. You're like a Casio keyboard that's been given the gift of language. Sort of.

Brake tappers. I'm really enjoying the stick figure rendering of you and your kids on the back window of your Honda Odyssey. Don't spoil it.

Spazzes who go on a reality show and start a sentence: "I'm a Christian, so . . ." After years of detailed anthropological study, I can report, with a fairly high degree of certainty, that what you're about to say will be certifiably crazy.

This might be entertaining if I weren't a Christian myself. But I am.

And you're a big reason people just judged me for saying that.

The Foundation for a Better Life. Your TV spots actually make me want to be a worse person.

**Grown man riding a skateboard down
the sidewalk.** Slow down—your parents' basement
isn't going anywhere.

Patriot wearing the Declaration of Independence as a polo shirt. Ahh, the Fourth of July, when you honor our country by pit-staining a polyester-cotton blend reproduction of one of its most significant pieces of history.

Broadcasters who say "we" and/or call players by their first names. Remember how you weren't cool enough to hang with them in high school? Hasn't changed.

Flies. If my biggest selling point were that I ate dead stuff, I'd probably try to be a little more inconspicuous.

AT&T. Phew. Your text recommending I add a voice-mail password made it through just before my phone didn't ring and went straight to voicemail.

Movie critics. How's it feel to make a living being critical of everything you see? Seriously, I want to know. It seems pretty sweet.

Professors who respond to a detailed e-mail in three words or less. Any issue worth raising can be addressed thoroughly with a lowercase "yes."

Baristas who hear "nonfat vanilla latte" and translate that to "skinny vanilla latte." There are at least five things about this complaint that are making me less manly—a dangerous game considering I wasn't exactly in Chuck Norris territory to begin with.

And you know what? I don't care.

That's how gross sugar-free vanilla is.

Vegans. Vegetarians are pretty cool with me. But I'm fairly certain you're actively rooting for my chicken to be undercooked.

Rider Strong. Many think of you as Shawn Hunter from *Boy Meets World*. I think of you as having the best non-porn porn name ever.

Teenagers who don't get zits. At 15, I thought I simply had bad luck—the kind that had prepared me to at least minor in whitehead-popping techniques by the time I went off to college. Now I'm in my 30s with a receding hairline. And guess who still has clearer skin than me?

Yes, it's like, you, you little Proactiv-takin' bastards.

Sneezy waiter. I want to believe you cover your mouth with your sleeve each time. I also want to believe I wasn't the only one at my wedding who thought I had moves like Usher.

Entitled Nordstrom shopper. Threatening the salesman after he accidentally bumped you doesn't complement your Botox.

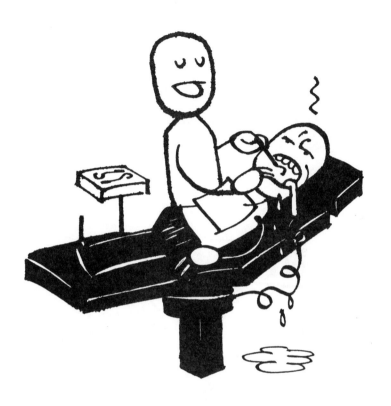

Hygienists who ask questions with their hands in our mouths. You: "Excited for the new season of *Project Runway*?" Us: "Bcgh tfg." You: "Me too."

People who get their teeth whitened at a kiosk in the mall. Had this technology existed in 1492, Columbus wouldn't have needed stars to navigate; he could've followed your glowing mouth across the Atlantic straight to the New World.

Brownnosers. Imagining someone who literally has poop on his nose isn't as gross as watching you ask your boss about his Lexus.

Josh Lucas. Casting Executive 1: "We've got a problem. McConaughey would be perfect, but he's not available. If only there were a 'poor man's Matthew McConaughey.'"

Casting Executive 2: "Josh Lucas?"

Casting Executive 1: "That'll work."

Captain Obvious. Let me get this straight: I *shouldn't* have run over that rock with the lawnmower? If only you had been here five minutes ago.

Celebrities who "confess" to getting a boob job. Are you saying your chest *didn't* just swell from all the love filling your heart?

Guys who go out of their way to say that they've never seen porn. You're lying. Unless you're Amish.

***Star* magazine.** Fact-checking is for nerds.

Creepy hypnotists. My bad. That was redundant.

Charlie Brown. Dealing with male pattern baldness at age eight is hard. But if you don't respect yourself, Lucy never will, either.

**People who flip through this book
in the store and then put it back.**

Let's cut the crap: You don't like me, I don't like you.
See you outside.

Acknowledgments

So many people to thank, so painfully obvious how fast you run out of synonyms for doing it.

Thank you first and foremost to my wife, Jenny, for keeping her cool despite constantly being asked: "Is this funny?" And for tolerating my dictionary collection.

Much love to mom and dad for investing so much in my education and then still speaking to me after I decided to pin my hopes on a Twitter feed.

Big ups to Sheila, Rein, Susan, Kate, Joey, and Keith for not giving me any reasons to write in-law jokes.

Mad props to my agent, Marissa, for allowing me to start sentences with "My agent," and to everyone at Adams, especially Brendan and Diane, for turning me into an "author."

Muchas gracias a Ryan por sus excepcionales ilustraciones. (Y a Adela por verificar mi español.)

A knowing nod goes to Aunt Lia, Uncle John, Cola, Laurie, Terry, Michael, Sean, Charlie, Nihar, Molly, Brian, Erin, Tim, Joyce, Josh, Dennis, Warren, and Buckner for being awesome for reals.

I also have to say "what up" to all my friends on Twitter for spreading the word about this book and @KnowWhosAwesome.

Last but not least, a shout-out to my roommates from Notre Dame, without whom I would not understand the comedic potential of a four-inch-tall clown statue.

Ted Fox (South Bend, Indiana) counts being called "the perfect wiseass" by his wife's uncle as one of his biggest accomplishments. When he's not tweeting about how un-awesome people can be (@KnowWhos Awesome), he tries to maintain employment at his alma mater, Notre Dame.

Ryan Hannus (Boston, Massachusetts) is a freelance illustrator and a full-time special ed teacher. He enjoys drawing his friends, primates, and trees.